S.O.A.P.

HOW TO CLEAN UP YOUR *STINKING THINKING* ONE DAY AT A TIME

SALLY STIERHOFF

WestBow
PRESS

A DIVISION OF THOMAS NELSON

WestBow Press books may be ordered through booksellers or by contacting:

WestBow Press
A Division of Thomas Nelson
1663 Liberty Drive
Bloomington, IN 47403
www.westbowpress.com
1-(866) 928-1240

ISBN: 978-1-4497-9283-1 (sc)
ISBN: 978-1-4497-9282-4 (e)

Library of Congress Control Number: 2013907542

Printed in the United States of America.

WestBow Press rev. date: 6/27/2013

"Let's be honest, life is very messy and complicated at times. We all know this to be true. Weaving our way through these trying times is a daunting task for even the most spiritually stalwart person. This book by Sally Stierhoff is an excellent spiritual exercise which can strengthen you for those times when life seems more than you can handle. Regardless of where you are in your faith walk with God, you will benefit from the time you spend immersed in this book."

Pastor Tim Reeves, Middleburg United Methodist Church

"I have found that using Sally's devotional guide is a great tool in getting started doing the S.O.A.P. method described in the book written by Wayne Cordeiro, "The Divine Mentor". She has taken the next step with thoughtful Bible scripture and reading examples, to establish a fresh new approach for anyone wanting a deeper relationship and knowledge of God's word and answers to their everyday lives. I would highly recommend this devotional."

Kevin Mabry, Gospel Music Evangelist and Recording Artist

Half of the proceeds from all the profits from the sales of this book will be used to print and distribute copies free of charge for use in outreach ministries throughout the world.

For more information visit the author's website at: www.sallystierhoff.com

THIS BOOK BELONGS TO:

Dedication

I would like to dedicate this book to the memory of my parents, Ralph and Bea Hardman, whose faith and love guided, protected, and encouraged me. They loved people deeply, and their faith in the Lord was evident in every aspect of their life. They loved the Bible. They each had a Bible that was worn, written in, and falling apart, just as mine is now. My father loved the Bible so much that he bought and passed out over 10,000 mini Bibles. He numbered each Bible so he could remember how many he gave away. I remember when I was younger I laughed about it, but now that I am older I understand my parents and their faith. I have to say, I could not be more proud of two people.

When it comes down to it, our life is really not about our accomplishments or what we own. Our life is about how much we love and how we treat people. It is about whether our faith sits on a shelf with all the other dusty books, or if we live it on our knees praying and demonstrating love in our homes, communities, or wherever we find ourselves.

I can just imagine the Lord saying to my parents when they went home to be with Him, "Well done, good and faithful servants. Because of you, my love for the human race continues on in the lives of all the people you have touched."

Preface

A few years ago a friend gave me a book that changed my life by teaching me a new and brilliant technique of Bible study through journaling. By journaling through the Bible with this method, I have improved many areas of my life including my relationships and my feelings about myself. When I find something so incredible, I become motivated to share it. After a while, I began to think about how I could use this method of journaling to create a 30 day devotional to inspire and encourage others.

The quirky title of the book came to me when I began to see changes in myself that made me happy. I began to notice the dark cloud of ugly feelings start to leave my mind and peace and joy take its place. I had already referred to my thoughts as stinking thinking, and it was the S.O.A.P. method of journaling that was clearing it away, so the title of this book came easily to me.

Our thoughts precede our actions. If we have a mind full of stinking thinking, there is a very good chance that we will do something that will cause us to suffer grave consequences. Many times the consequences themselves propel us into changing; other times we are unable to remove the ugly feelings and thoughts from our mind.

This devotional contains subjects that touch on many reasons for our stinking thinking and other subjects that reveal the great love and gifts God has for His children. I have prayed and studied the scriptures to provide the ones that I believe will begin to improve a person's life in 30 days. Just as a body needs nourishment every day, a mind must be fed positive spiritual food daily or it will find unhealthy thoughts return.

This book is not only about journaling. It is about starting a journey with endless possibilities that can rejuvenate a person's life and fill it with love and peace. It is definitely a journey worth taking.

Acknowledgment

One of the most amazing books I have read is by *Wayne Cordeiro, The Devine Mentor, Bloomington, Minnesota, Bethany House Publishers*. I especially love this quote from his book, **"Wisdom teaches you the lesson before you make the mistake. On the other hand, consequences demand that you make the mistake first."** In his book, Wayne teaches us how to obtain wisdom and change our life for the better. He developed the S.O.A.P. method that I have used in this book. I am very grateful to Wayne for his literary contribution and for his permission to use excerpts from his book to write this devotional.

For proofreading and/or reviewing this manuscript, I would like to thank, Wayne, John, Mark, Debbie, Shelly, Pastor Tim, Sue, Joyce, Kevin and Kim. Your suggestions and help were invaluable.

I would especially like to thank my Heavenly Father, because with Him all things **are** possible.

Introduction

Stinking Thinking

I know something about stinking thinking. It is that awful thought process that contains any or all of the following emotions: anger, doubt, despair, jealousy, hatred, fear and self-pity. It sneaks up on all of us at times in our lives. It may be because of a terrible situation we find ourselves in, a consequence of a poor decision, or something imposed upon us by others. It may also be, as in my case, brought on by health issues that go on far too long. I found myself in despair, fed up and in pain, and that is when my stinking thinking would start. This is the thought process of "I'm mad at the world, and I'm sick of everything." I eventually got to the point where I realized that this type of thinking was only making me feel worse. Where can I go from here, I wondered? I tried everything humanly possible and spent quite a bit of money without success. All along God was there waiting patiently to lift me up out of my despair and fill me with love and hope. He was willing to forgive me and set my mind free. All I had to do was pray for His help.

What I have learned is that stinking thinking is like an illness in our mind. It never gets better unless we start to feed it good stuff from God's word that helps it heal. When individuals allow themselves to meditate on God's word and pray, they soon begin to feel the despair lift. The joy comes back into their lives, and they notice that the stinking thinking begins to leave.

God made us with a desire to commune with Him. When we live a life without Him, we feel as though we are missing something. We try everything to make ourselves happy, but we cannot fill the void. We make poor choices that lead to serious consequences that lead to despair. God sent His son Jesus to be born on earth and live as a human so that he would experience the pain, emotions, and struggles that humans do. He understood us and chose to die a horrible, painful death on the cross. He bore our sins so that we might have eternal life. Making a change is as easy as praying, "Lord Jesus, come into my heart, forgive my sins, and help me change my life. Amen."

Now forget the past. If you prayed that prayer, and meant it, you are forgiven. You are now on your way to clearing your mind and becoming a happier person who will enjoy making other people happy.

This 30-day devotional uses the S.O.A.P. method: S-Scripture, O-Observation, A-Application, and P-Prayer. After doing this daily Bible reading and journaling, I felt a spirit of anxiety lift from me and joy and peace take its place. It has been wonderful. This method of going through the Bible is more than just reading words; it is an interactive way of thinking, writing and asking God to speak to us through His word. It is amazing how much more a person can comprehend from studying the Bible with this method.

My intent in writing this devotional is to start you on a journey of your own through God's word. This journey can move you from despair to hope, from death to eternal life, and from stinking thinking to joyful peace as you clean away the dirt of the past.

How to Begin

Take a few minutes before you start your day. Get comfortable and pray for God to reveal something new and fresh to you through His word. Start by reading this daily devotional that uses the S.O.A.P. method. You will then see on the next page a segment of scripture to read and a Bible verse for you to do yourself. I call this your Personal S.O.A.P.

When you are ready to begin on your own with your Bible, start by purchasing a good journaling binder to keep your entries together. You will want to refer to your journal entries later. Start reading your Bible. Begin with the New Testament by reading a few verses or a whole chapter at a time. Pick out a few key verses that caught your attention while you were reading. Write the Bible verses down under, "S" (Scripture), then write, "O" (Observation), what you think these verses of scripture mean. Follow this with, "A" (Application), write down how you can apply this to your own life. Finally, P (Prayer), write a prayer asking the Lord to help you use what you just learned. You can also use this method doing a daily Bible reading program. For example, the one I have on my e-book is _The One Year Bible_, New Living Translation, Carol Stream, Illinois, Tyndale House Publishers, Inc. This book has the Old and New Testament passages together for daily reading. Also, I would certainly recommend that you pick up a copy of Wayne's book, _The Devine Mentor_, Bloomington, Minnesota, Bethany House Publishers. It will truly bless you with his understanding of the Bible and human nature.

Now that you are equipped to start your own incredible life journal, jump in, get your feet wet, and go out and tackle the world with a smile knowing that God is by your side.

Enjoy the Journey.

God Bless,

Your Sister in Christ,

Sally

ABILITY

Scripture

Philippians 4:13

I can do all things through Christ who strengthens me. (21c KJV)

Observation

All things. Wow! Through Christ I have the power to accomplish what I need to do, the ability to do what I want, and the strength to get through it all. This is my favorite Bible verse, and it is so good to read it again. When I am having a difficult time with people, my job or an illness, this is the verse to remember. God is with me. I can do extraordinary things believing and reciting this Bible verse. I remember in my decorative painting business, sometimes a client would ask for a particular type of artwork. I would recite this Bible verse in my head and I was able to do remarkable things. When I went through health issues and the death of my parents, I would recite this verse. This verse has changed my life and carried me through many difficult situations.

Application

Memorizing and reciting this Bible verse is a good habit to develop. It is a promise from God. I need to use it and believe it with my whole heart and share it with others. I need to try something new for God without being afraid. He is my strength and He will help me through everything. I need to change my mind from fear to confidence and walk in faith.

Prayer

Lord, I need you day and night, for where I am weak you are strong. Help me to stand firm on your promise. Help me to overcome fear, doubt, and criticism from other people. I praise you for your mercy and for your strength. Thank you for the incredible things you are going to help me accomplish in your name.

In Jesus' name,

Amen

ABILITY

Personal S.O.A.P.

Read Deuteronomy 8:17-20

<u>Scripture</u>

Deuteronomy 8:18

But remember the Lord your God, for it is he who gives the ability to produce wealth, and so confirms his covenant, which he swore to your ancestors, as it is today. (NIV)

<u>Observation</u>

<u>Application</u>

<u>Prayer</u>

ANGER

James 1:19-21

My dear brothers, take note of this: Everyone should be quick to listen, slow to speak and slow to become angry, for man's anger does not bring about the righteous life that God desires. Therefore, get rid of all moral filth and the evil that is so prevalent and humbly accept the word planted in you, which can save you. (NIV)

Observation

Anger is something I witness every day. There are many people filled with anger, and they cannot have a normal, peaceful life. They are in stores, on the road, and many times in our homes. Also, there is a lot of anger and violence on TV and in video games. Anger almost seems acceptable until it is directed at me. When I am really upset about something, I find it very hard to keep from sinning, which reminds me of another Bible verse.

Proverbs 29:22. *An angry man stirs up dissension, and a hot tempered one commits many sins.*

Sometimes a person can get so mad that the anger takes on a life of its own, and the person can no longer control it. Quick to listen and slow to speak means that I must take the time to try to understand what people are saying and not jump to the conclusion that I already know their intent. How can I possibly know what is on someone else's mind or the meaning of every word they speak? I may never understand what experience they are going through to bring about their actions. I could be the most devoted Christian anyone has ever seen, but when I let my anger take over I forfeit my integrity. This behavior does not *bring about the righteous life that God desires.* My anger inevitably hurts those around me. Anger can break up friendships or families. It can cause people to break the law and ruin their lives. Anger about sin is much different from anger that sins. I can be angry about injustice, oppression, and evil offenses, but I must be careful how I direct it. It is okay to speak out against evil, but I must do it in a respectful manner, letting God direct my actions.

Application

I need to take the time to listen, process, and ask questions about what people are saying to try to understand them. If they truly mean to be rude, I need to let it go, walk away, and give it to God. I cannot let someone else's sin cause me to sin and upset my life. Time spent on anger is time without peace. I must resist the temptation to fall into a trap and get snared by sinful and destructive behavior. How can I clean up my life and become a happier person if I let anger control me, instead of controlling it with God's help? I must memorize scripture.

Prayer

Lord, you know my weaknesses. Help me be strong, patient, loving and kind. Help me to resist the temptation to lash out at others. Fill me with a calm and gentle spirit that loves people as you love them. Help me to be quick to listen and slow to get angry. Give me discernment, so that I might have an understanding of each situation and a clear picture of what my actions should be. Help me to extend forgiving grace to others just as you have shown to me.

In Jesus' name,

Amen

ANGER

Personal S.O.A.P.

Read Proverbs 15:1-4

Scripture

Proverbs 15:1

A gentle answer turns away wrath, but a harsh word stirs up anger. (NIV)

Observation

Application

Prayer

ANXIETY

Scripture

Philippians 4:4-7

Rejoice in the Lord always. I will say it again: Rejoice! Let your gentleness be evident to all. The Lord is near. Do not be anxious about anything, but in everything, by prayer and petition, with thanksgiving, present your request to God. And the peace of God, which transcends all understanding, will guard your hearts and your minds in Christ Jesus. (NIV)

Observation

Rejoice. Webster's dictionary describes it as: to be glad, delighted, full of joy. I need to rejoice by being thankful. Let me praise the Lord in my prayers, my songs and express joy to other people. This verse says it twice so I know this is an important aspect of my faith. How can my faith be dull when I am full of joy? I must be kind and gentle to those around me. In other words, I need to be pleasant to be around, not grumbling, complaining or bitter. The Lord is always with me. I can pray in my mind as well as with my voice. I can pray wherever I am. With thanksgiving, I can present my requests to God. I should be thankful for what He has already provided, but also thank God for things that have not yet happened. When I give thanks for what I pray for before they happen, then I believe they will come to pass. The faith I develop from that belief will give me peace as God increases my understanding, which will help protect my thoughts and emotions.

Application

Attitude adjustment comes to my mind. Life is short. I need to live in joy and be pleasant and fun to be around. I want to live with a thankful attitude, rejoicing when I pray. I need to give my anxieties to God because He can handle them, whereas I cannot. I need to ask the Holy Spirit to fill me with wisdom and understanding. My goal should be to relax and enjoy my life.

<u>Prayer</u>

Lord, why do I try to handle all these things by myself? It's too much for me. The anxiety of it all makes me sad and unhappy. This is not the way I want to live. I praise you Lord and thank you for dying on the cross to set me free from the chains of sin and the prison of poisonous emotions. I thank you for all the wonderful people in my life and all that you have provided me. I am grateful for all that you are going to do for me and how you will guide me. Take my burdens and fill me with your joy and peace.

In Jesus' name,

Amen

ANXIETY ▮▮▮▮▮▮▮▮▮▮▮▮▮▮▮▮▮▮▮▮▮▮▮▮

Personal S.O.A.P.

Read Psalm 28:6-9

Scripture

Psalm 28:7

The Lord is my strength and my shield; my heart trusts in him, and he helps me. My heart leaps for joy, and with my song I praise him. (NIV)

Observation

Application

Prayer

BEHAVIOR

Galatians 5:22-26

But the fruit of the Spirit is love, joy, peace, patience, kindness, goodness, faithfulness, gentleness and self-control. Against such things there is not law. Those who belong to Christ Jesus have crucified the sinful nature with its passions and desires. Since we live by the Spirit, let us keep in step with the Spirit. Let us not become conceited, provoking and envying each other. (NIV)

Observation

The fruit that grows from the vine reflects how good the plant is and what kind of soil, water and food it receives. The same is true for me. My behavior (my fruit) reflects my spiritual life on the inside which is my connection to God. If I stay connected in worship and prayer, then my fruit is good. If I drift away, then my fruit may reflect a more sinful nature that acts upon undesirable behavior. This is behavior that I do not like in other people, but behavior that I am too weak to resist on my own. True strength is in the Lord. When I stay in fellowship with God, I am at peace. I am happy and in control. I find that people see the difference and enjoy being around me. I may like my new self so well that I could become conceited as though I did this on my own. If I were truthful, I would realize that only by the grace of God did I get a do-over, and only by His love was I redeemed.

Actions

I must remember that when I get too busy for God it is very easy for me to fall into sin and revert to my ugly behavior. I cannot forget where I came from so that I can remind myself that I do not want to be that way any longer. I must cling to what is good, right, and true and believe, study, and pray. I need to spend time with positive people, listen to Christian radio, and watch shows with better morals.

Prayer

Lord, thank you for delivering me from my sinful self. Even though I never did any of the things many people think of as terribly sinful, my behavior was. My actions were ugly and mean at times. I wish I could take back some of the things I said in the past, but I cannot. I am so glad you forgave my sins and set me free so I can move forward in peace to start a better life with you.

In Jesus' name,

Amen

BEHAVIOR

Personal S.O.A.P.

Read Ephesians 4:17-32

<u>Scripture</u>

Ephesians 4:29-32

Do not let any unwholesome talk come out of your mouths, but only what is helpful for building others up according to their needs, that it may benefit those who listen. And do not grieve the Holy Spirit of God, with whom you were sealed for the day of redemption. Get rid of all bitterness, rage and anger, brawling and slander, along with every form of malice. Be kind and compassionate to one another, forgiving each other, just as in Christ God forgave you. (NIV)

<u>Observation</u>

<u>Actions</u>

<u>Prayer</u>

COURAGE

Scripture

Joshua 1:5-6

No one will be able to stand up against you all the days of your life. As I was with Moses, so I will be with you; I will never leave you nor forsake you. Be strong and courageous, because you will lead these people to inherit the land I swore to their forefathers to give them. (NIV)

Observation

Courage is one of those words that come to mind when I think of soldiers. I must have the courage every day to stand up for what I believe and to do what I know is right. It takes a considerable amount of courage to say no to temptation and walk away. Sometimes I do not have that much strength within me. God's promises are true, and He promised that He would never leave me or forsake me. On the other hand, God does not push His way into my life. I must desire a relationship with Him and ask for His help. Soldiers get medals for their courage, but I will receive the ultimate award promised to me, and that is a home in heaven.

Application

I need to pray for courage and believe in God's promise that He will never leave me. I must practice courage, and with each struggle I will become stronger for the next. I need to look back on my victories and gain confidence knowing that God was there to see me through.

Prayer

Lord, help me face each day remembering you are with me and that I have nothing to fear. Help me to remember all the times you saw me through tough situations. Lord, help the memory of those times build on my confidence so that I can face every day with anticipation instead of worry. Thank you, Lord.

In Jesus' name,

Amen

COURAGE

Personal S.O.A.P.

Read Joshua 1:7-9

<u>Scripture</u>

Joshua 1:9

Have I not commanded you? Be strong and courageous. Do not be afraid; do not be discouraged, for the Lord your God will be with you wherever you go. (NIV)

<u>Observation</u>

<u>Application</u>

<u>Prayer</u>

DOING GOOD

Scripture

James 4:17

Anyone, then, who knows the good he ought to do and doesn't do it, sins. (NIV)

Observation

When I see a need, and I am physically or financially able to help, but refuse, this verse clearly says I sin. This truly changes what I have thought all along about sin. I believed sin was only lying, cheating, murder, and so on. How wrong I was.

Where there is a need, God calls me to help; to be His hands and feet in this world. I can help with whatever ability I have, whether it is to help with my hands and feet, or to share my money to cover a need or both. Maybe I can cook a little extra or just be a friend who can listen and pray. The needs are endless, but the workers are few. As a believer in Christ, I am called to do good works.

Application

I need to pray and volunteer, or share some of the financial blessings God has provided me. I always need to be a friend and prayer partner, and show compassion.

Prayer

Lord, you have given me so much and taken such good care of me. Show me where I can do good work with what I have to make a difference in this world. Please let your love show through me. Forgive me for those times I chose not to help and sinned against you.

In Jesus' name,

Amen

DOING GOOD

Personal S.O.A.P.

Read James 2:14-26

James 2:16-17

If one of you says to them, "Go in peace; keep warm and well fed," but does nothing about their physical needs, what good is it? In the same way, faith by itself, if it is not accompanied by action, is dead. (NIV)

Observation

Application

Prayer

EVIL

Scripture

Ephesians 6:10-12

Finally, be strong in the Lord and in his mighty power. Put on the full armor of God so that you can take your stand against the devil's schemes. For our struggle is not against flesh and blood, but against the rulers, against the authorities, against the powers of this dark world and against the spiritual forces of evil in the heavenly realms. (NIV)

Observation

I am not merely a human, but a spiritual being who is constantly under attack. My mind struggles with good and evil all day long. I make good decisions and then poor decisions. I say and do things that hurt other people, and then I feel deep regret. I am weak by myself, and the consequences of my actions sometimes last a long time. God has provided me with protection from the attack, and that protection is the Bible. When I read and study it, I fill my mind with uplifting spiritual guidance, so when the attack comes I know how to defend myself. I think being strong in the Lord means I must be involved with the Lord, by praying and allowing my thoughts to be of Him.

Application

I must stand firm in my faith and fill my mind with scripture so that nothing can steal my peace from me. The words of the Bible are powerful and full of love. They will shield me when the threats come, and the temptation is overwhelming. I need to pray for the strength to overcome and command the powers of evil to leave in Jesus' name.

Prayer

Lord, I am tired and weary. I need your strength. Let your word bring meaning and understanding to me. Help me to memorize your scripture so that I can fight the good fight and stand my ground against the forces of evil. Give me compassion for others, and help me to remember that we are all in a battle every day. Thank you for your word.

In Jesus' name,

Amen

EVIL

Personal S.O.A.P.

Read James 1:12-18

Scripture

James 1:13-15

When tempted, no one should say, "God is tempting me." For God cannot be tempted by evil, nor does He tempt anyone; but each person is tempted when they are dragged away by their own evil desire and enticed. Then, after desire has conceived, it gives birth to sin; and sin, when it is full-grown, gives birth to death. (NIV)

Observation

Application

Prayer

WEEKLY REFLECTIONS

Key thoughts from this week's devotions.

DAY 1

_____
_____
_____

DAY 2

_____
_____
_____

DAY 3

_____
_____
_____

DAY 4

_____
_____
_____

DAY 5

_____
_____
_____

DAY 6

_____
_____
_____

DAY 7

_____
_____
_____

FAVORITISM

Scripture

James 2:1-8

My brothers, as believers in our glorious Lord Jesus Christ, do not show favoritism. Suppose a man comes into your meeting wearing a gold ring and fine clothes, and a poor man in shabby clothes also comes in. If you show special attention to the man wearing fine clothes and say, "Here's a good seat for you," but say to the poor man, "You stand there" or "Sit on the floor by my feet," have you not discriminated among yourselves and become judges with evil thoughts? Listen, my dear brothers: Has not God chosen those who are poor in the eyes of the world to be rich in faith and to inherit the kingdom he promised those who love him? But you have insulted the poor. Is it not the rich who are exploiting you? Are they not the ones who are dragging you into court? Are they not the ones who are slandering the name of him to whom you belong? If you really keep the royal law found in Scripture, "Love your neighbor as yourself," you are doing right. (NIV)

Observation

Passing judgment on people because of their appearance, where they live, or even what type of job they have is not the way God wants me to be. In the eyes of God, all people are equal with the same opportunity to love Him and other people. By looking at a person, I have no way of knowing what is in their heart. I can only see their outward appearance; the shell of a person, not the spirit of a person. I believe that God chose the poor to inherit his kingdom because they put God first in their lives. They do not have materialistic distractions. They put all their trust in God while some people may love money more than God. I think I may also judge the wealthy as well. Having money and using it for the glory of God is what I am called to do. I believe God gave me a talent that helped me make money to further his work on this earth. It is up to me to make the right decisions with whatever God provides. I should never fool myself into thinking that I am better than anyone else because of what I possess or what talents I have received.

Application

    I need to pray that God will give me a heart for all people. I must do my best every day to see people as God sees them; not poor or rich, by race, by their job, or even by their education. I must resist the temptation to think that I am better than anyone else. I must strive to treat people fairly and with respect and let God's love show through me. I need to make it a goal to love other people as I love myself.

Prayer

    Lord, forgive me when I look at another and judge them in my heart. Help me to be fair, and to free my mind of all the garbage that has filtered through me over the years that has caused me to form harmful opinions. I know you change lives and that it is your job to judge; not mine. Help me to change, and show me ways that I can show love to all those around me.

In Jesus' name,

Amen

FAVORITISM ▰▰▰▰▰▰▰▰▰▰

Personal S.O.A.P.

Read Romans 15:1-7

Scripture

Romans 15:5-7

May the God who gives endurance and encouragement give you a spirit of unity among yourselves as you follow Christ Jesus, so that with one heart and mouth you may glorify the God and Father of our Lord Jesus Christ. Accept one another, then just as Christ accepted you, in order to bring praise to God. (NIV)

Observation

Application

Prayer

FORGIVENESS

Scripture

Matthew 6:14-15

For if you forgive men when they sin against you, your heavenly father will also forgive you. But if you do not forgive men their sins, your Father will not forgive your sins. (NIV)

Observation

This Bible verse is rarely talked about even though it is clearly stated in the Lord's Prayer, Matthew 6:12 "Forgive us our debts, as we also have forgiven our debtors."

This verse is powerful because it is so straightforward. If I carry grudges and refuse to forgive people, then my heavenly Father will not forgive my sins. What I have learned is that un-forgiveness hurts me more than it hurts the person that has offended me. It becomes a disease in me that poisons my attitude, my actions, and the way I speak and treat people. Un-forgiveness can be all consuming. It robs me of my joy, my peace of mind, and my relationship with the Lord. Perhaps the whole point of this verse is this: If I have un-forgiveness in my heart I will continue to sin and destroy my future. It also shows me that if I do not forgive others I am not serious enough about my relationship with Christ to lay it down and move on with my life.

Application

I must make an effort to forgive people with God's help, in prayer, soon after the offense has taken place. I must realize that maybe there are reasons that people act the way they do. I need to make it a practice to tell God my hurt, pain, and anger, and let Him help me through it. I may not have to be around those people very often, but I must forgive them.

Prayer

Lord, help me work through my disappointment and anger, and fill me with your love and understanding. As I pray saying I forgive them, transform my heart and my mind. Forgive me of my sins, Lord Jesus, and grant me peace.

In Jesus' name,

Amen

FORGIVENESS

Personal S.O.A.P.

Read Mark 11:22-25

<u>Scripture</u>

Mark 11:24-25

Therefore I tell you, whatever you ask for in prayer, believe that you have received it, and it will be yours. And when you stand praying, if you hold anything against anyone, forgive them, so that your Father in heaven may forgive you your sins. (NIV)

Luke 23:34

Jesus said "Father, forgive them, for they do not know what they are doing." (NIV)

<u>Observation</u>

<u>Application</u>

<u>Prayer</u>

GRACE

Ephesians 2:8-10

For it is by grace you have been saved, through faith and this not from yourselves, it is the gift of God-not by works, so that no one can boast. For we are God's workmanship, created in Christ Jesus to do good works, which God prepared in advance for us to do. (NIV)

Observation

The dictionary defines grace as mercy or clemency. I have been given an incredible gift; a gift I cannot earn or buy. It is the gift of eternal life, and it is God's gift to me through Jesus Christ. It is like a gift offered to me by a friend. I have the choice to accept it or refuse it, but it is freely given. Jesus paid the price for the sins of mankind, and He is asking me to share eternity with Him. By receiving His grace, I receive the perfect gift. I not only change the course of my future, but I also change my life for the better. By inviting Jesus into my heart, I begin a relationship that strengthens me and helps me become a confident person full of joy.

Application

I must ask Jesus into my heart to receive this incredible gift of grace. I need to unload my baggage of guilt and shame because I know that Jesus paid the ultimate price for them. I will look forward not back. Starting today, I will begin to study and pray; refresh my mind and spirit.

Prayer

Lord Jesus, come into my life and forgive my sins. I accept your gift of forgiving grace, and I want to begin a relationship with you. Guide me and show me the way to free my mind of the past as I start a new life.

In Jesus' name,

Amen

GRACE

Personal S.O.A.P.

Read John 3:13-21

Scripture

John 3:16-17

For God so loved the world that he gave his one and only son, that whoever believes in him shall not perish but have eternal life. For God did not send his Son into the world to condemn the world but to save the world through him. (NIV)

Observation

Application

Prayer

GREATEST COMMANDMENT

Matthew 22:36-40

"Teacher, which is the greatest commandment in the Law?" Jesus replied; "Love the Lord your God with all your heart and with all your soul and with all your mind'. This is the first and greatest commandment. And the second is like it; 'Love your neighbor as yourself.' All the Law and the Prophets hang on these two commandments." (NIV)

Observation

To love God with my heart, soul, and mind, means that I would regard God above myself. As I go through my busy life I must ask myself, how much time do I actually think about God? How much time do I spend in prayer, reading the Bible, or in worship? If a mother or father makes the statement that they love their children but then they do not call them or go see them, what does that say? It is the same with God. Do I really love Him? My actions will show the truth about me.

His second commandment is to love my neighbor as much as I love myself. I believe He is saying that everyone around me should be just as valuable to me as I am to myself. If I love and do for myself, then I should be able to do for other people. I should be friendly and caring so that everyone can see God's love in me.

Application

I need to get up in the morning and start my day off with God in prayer and Bible study. I want to create a habit of meditating on God with a spirit of gratitude. I must get real with myself about the areas in my life that I need to change and ask God for help. I should start by watching less TV and spending more time with family, neighbors, friends, and church members. I need to take the time to help people in need; share love and make friendships.

Prayer

Lord, forgive me for not putting you first in my life. Help me see myself as I really am, and give me the strength to make the necessary changes. You created me, and you know what is best for me. Help me to give up my stubborn selfish ways and let you guide me into the incredible life you have planned for me. Help me to care for others as well as I care for myself. Open my heart and fill it with your love.

In Jesus' name,

Amen

GREATEST COMMANDMENT ▰▰▰▰

Personal S.O.A.P.

Read Exodus 20:1-17

<u>Scripture</u>

Exodus 20:2-3

"I am the LORD your God, who brought you out of Egypt, out of the land of slavery. You shall have no other gods before me." (NIV)

<u>Observation</u>

<u>Application</u>

<u>Prayer</u>

HAPPINESS

Scripture

Ecclesiastes 2:26

To the person who pleases him, God gives wisdom, knowledge and happiness, but to the sinner he gives the task of gathering and storing up wealth to hand it over to the one who pleases God. This too is meaningless, a chasing after the wind. (NIV)

Observation

By establishing a relationship with the living God through Jesus Christ, and by following his example to love one another, I am pleasing God. When I live this way, I will not hurt or harm people with my actions. On the contrary, I will want to develop good relationships. When I do the things that please God, I create an environment of harmony and peace where God can give me wisdom and happiness. Living apart from God is more about living a life centered on self and material possessions. I find myself chasing after something that never gives me that deep down peace and fulfillment. God created me with a place for Him in my soul that only He can fill. That is why I will never find genuine happiness without Him.

Application

I need to invite God into my everyday life, not just when I am in trouble and have nowhere to turn. I must practice pleasing Him instead of myself so that I can find peace and happiness, and develop good relationships. I need to let God handle things so I can live by trusting instead of worrying. In this way, I will be free to be happy and content with what He provides.

Prayer

Lord, give me the desire to serve you and please you. Fill me with your wisdom as I go through my day trusting you and being thankful so that I can find happiness.

In Jesus' name,

Amen

HAPPINESS ▰▰▰▰▰▰▰▰▰▰▰▰

Personal S.O.A.P.

Read Ecclesiastes 3:1-12

<u>Scripture</u>

Ecclesiastes 3:11-12

He has made everything beautiful in its time. He has also set eternity in the human heart; yet no one can fathom what God has done from beginning to end. I know that there is nothing better for people than to be happy and to do good while they live. (NIV)

<u>Observation</u>

<u>Application</u>

<u>Prayer</u>

HARMONY

Scripture

I Peter 3:8-12

Finally, all of you, live in harmony with one another; be sympathetic, love as brothers, be compassionate and humble. Do not repay evil with evil or insult with insult, but with blessing, because to this you were called so that you may inherit a blessing. For, "whoever would love life and see good days must keep his tongue from evil and his lips from deceitful speech. He must turn from evil and do good; he must seek peace and pursue it. For the eyes of the Lord are on the righteous and his ears are attentive to their prayer, but the face of the Lord is against those who do evil." (NIV)

Observation

I believe living in harmony means living in peace. A person cannot constantly be in turmoil with other people and have peace and health within their own bodies. All this brings me back to the golden rule which is found in: *Luke 6:31. Do to others as you would have them do to you.* If I do not want to be treated badly then I should not treat other people badly, because, for every action there is a reaction. Getting along well with other people helps me at home, at work, and in my community. By being kind, I become a person that people like to be around. If I am always complaining, bitter and offensive then people are not going to enjoy my company. If this would become a habit, then it would be hard to stop without God's help. To *seek peace and pursue it* would mean this takes work. With prayer, Bible study, and the fellowship of positive people, I can make the change. If I continue in a life of disharmony and sin, I am separated from God.

Application

I need to read and study the Bible, surround myself with positive people, and pray for forgiveness. I must begin to pray for God to make a change in the way I think and respond. I should spend time thinking about how I have been acting and the reasons for it. What could be the underlying cause of my discontent? I need to recognize the negative influences that I allow into my life and begin to fill my life with positive ones. I will begin to calm my mind and spirit by spending time enjoying the beauty in nature and appreciating the marvelous things God has provided.

Prayer

Lord, the years seem to go by and I don't even know how I got to be this way. Help me to change my thinking and my behavior, and bring me back to the person I was meant to be in you. Forgive me for being rude and only thinking about myself. Please help me to live in harmony with other people and find peace within.

In Jesus' name,

Amen

HARMONY

Personal S.O.A.P.

Read Romans 12:9-21

Scripture

Romans 12:12-16

Be joyful in hope, patient in affliction, faithful in prayer. Share with the Lord's people who are in need. Practice hospitality. Bless those who persecute you; bless and do not curse. Rejoice with those who rejoice; mourn with those who mourn. Live in harmony with one another. Do not be proud, but be willing to associate with people of low position. Do not be conceited. (NIV)

Observation

Application

Prayer

HATRED

Scripture

I John 4:20-21

Whoever claims to love God yet hates a brother or sister is a liar. For whoever does not love their brother and sister, whom they have seen, cannot love God, whom they have not seen. And he has given us this command: Anyone who loves God must also love their brother or sister. (NIV)

Observation

I cannot have hate in my heart and love God. I can hate evil and evil deeds, but I believe I must pray for other people not hate them. How can I demonstrate God's love to people if I have hate in my heart? How can I be at peace with myself if I have the fury of hate within me? Hate is a rage within me against another. It is a fire that burns slow and steady and some days out of control. I cannot enjoy the comfort of a fire unless I sit apart from it. In the same way, I cannot live in comfort and peace with the fire of hate burning inside me. Hate hurts me and my relationship with God.

Application

I need to confess my hate to God and ask Him to help me begin to deal with it. I must ask God to help me forgive those individuals who have offended me. I need to fill my mind with scripture and positive things to replace the negative hate. I must make an effort to seek out those individuals and make amends; show love and forgiveness. As always, I know that I need to pray often.

Prayer

Lord, help me work through this hate within me. Forgive me as I now forgive others in Jesus' name. Help me to understand myself and the buried reasons why I hate them. Help me clear this from my life and my mind. Fill me with love and forgiveness. Heal me Lord.

In Jesus' name,

Amen

HATRED

Personal S.O.A.P.

Read I John 2:3-11

<u>Scripture</u>

I John 2:9-10

Anyone who claims to be in the light but hates a brother or sister is still in the darkness. Anyone who loves their brother and sister lives in the light, and there is nothing in them to make them stumble. (NIV)

<u>Observation</u>

<u>Application</u>

<u>Prayer</u>

WEEKLY REFLECTIONS

Key thoughts from this week's devotions.

DAY 8

_____

_____

_____

DAY 9

_____

_____

_____

DAY 10

_____

_____

_____

DAY 11

_____

_____

_____

DAY 12

_____

_____

_____

DAY 13

_____

_____

_____

DAY 14

_____

_____

_____

HOLY SPIRIT ▟▟▟▟▟▟▟▟▟▟▟▟▟▟▟▟▟▟▟▟▟▟▟▟

I Corinthians 2:11-14

For who among men knows the thoughts of a man except the man's spirit within him? In the same way no one knows the thoughts of God except the Spirit of God. We have not received the spirit of the world but the Sprit who is from God, that we may understand what God has freely given us. This is what we speak, not in words taught us by human wisdom but in words taught by the Spirit, expressing spiritual truths in spiritual words. The man without the Sprit does not accept the things that come from the Spirit of God, for they are foolishness to him, and he cannot understand them because they are spiritually discerned. (NIV)

Observation

Jesus said in *John 14:26 But the Counselor, the Holy Spirit, whom the Father will send in my name, will teach you all things and will remind you of everything I have said to you.* The Holy Spirit is my telephone line to God. He is ever-present, communicating with God on my behalf. There is more than just the knowledge of the Holy Spirit. We must ask God to fill us with the Holy Spirit. *In Acts 8:15, it says: When they arrived, they prayed for them that they might receive the Holy Spirit, because the Holy Spirit had not yet come upon any of them, they had simply been baptized into the name of the Lord Jesus. (NIV)*

Without the Holy Spirit, I will not fully comprehend God's work in me or understand people who have received the Holy Spirit. In I Corinthians 2 it says a person that does not accept the Spirit will think all things that come from the Spirit of God are foolishness. The Holy Spirit is a gift from God to me for a better, more fulfilling life. The Holy Spirit changes my belief into a relationship with the Lord and my spirit into a receiver that processes God's thoughts and my prayers. The Holy Spirit will also guide and protect my thinking as it helps me to recognize the truth from a lie. When I live a life without the Holy Spirit, my faith is no more than the knowledge of God.

Application

    I need to ask God to fill me with His Spirit and refresh my mind every day. I must spend time reading His word and meditating. The dictionary says meditation is a solemn reflection on sacred matters as a devotional act or deep continued thought; reflection. I need to be in quiet thought, so I can receive what God is giving me through the Holy Spirit; praying and calming my mind, knowing God is in control.

Prayer

    Lord, fill me with your Holy Spirit and refresh my mind daily to help me understand your perfect will for my life. Give me guidance, grant me peace, and increase my faith as you work in me. Thank you for giving me your Spirit to guide and comfort me all day long.

In Jesus' name,

Amen

HOLY SPIRIT

Personal S.O.A.P.

Read John 14:15-20

Scripture

Jesus Promises the Holy Spirit

John 14:15-17

"If you love me, keep my commands. And I will ask the Father, and he will give you another advocate to help you and be with you forever—the Spirit of truth. The world cannot accept him, because it neither sees him nor knows him. But you know him, for he lives with you and will be in you." (NIV)

Observation

Application

Prayer

HOPE

Scripture

Isaiah 40:31

But those who hope in the LORD will renew their strength. They will soar on wings like eagles; they will run and not grow weary, they will walk and not be faint. (NIV)

Observation

Hope: to want and expect; trust and reliance. If I am to put my hope in the Lord, then I must believe, trust, and accept Him. I would have to overcome my fear and give up the control I feel I must have over every aspect of my life. If I am truly honest with myself, I can actually say that doing things on my own has not worked out so well. When I am able to relinquish my control, then the Lord will provide me the strength to rise above my challenges. To me, "Soar on wings like eagles" means, being able to see all the beauty in my everyday life and look above and beyond what's going on. In this way, I will have the strength to face adversity as I recognize my blessings and reap my rewards.

Application

I must trust in the Lord, not myself. He made me and He knows more than I what is best for me. I need to pray and be slow to take action; unlike the way I have responded in the past. I need to relax knowing that God is taking care of everything. I must rise above the negative and look for the positive. I need to do my part to make every situation better, knowing God will give me the strength.

Prayer

Lord, you made me in your own image and you created me from dust. I want to turn over my life to you and begin to trust you for everything. Guide me and free me of the burden of trying to handle everything on my own. I stand on your scripture that says you will renew my strength and help me rise above every situation. Help me see the true beauty in your creation and have the peace you promise me in your word.

In Jesus' name,

Amen

HOPE

Personal S.O.A.P.

Read Jeremiah 29:10-14

<u>Scripture</u>

Jeremiah 29:11-13

"For I know the plans I have for you," declares the Lord, "plans to prosper you and not to harm you, plans to give you hope and a future. Then you will call upon me and come and pray to me, and I will listen to you. You will seek me and find me when you seek me with all your heart." (NIV)

<u>Observation</u>

<u>Application</u>

<u>Prayer</u>

LOVE

I Corinthians 13:4-7

Love is patient, love is kind. It does not envy, it does not boast, it is not proud. It is not rude, it is not self-seeking, it is not easily angered, it keeps no record of wrongs. Love does not delight in evil but rejoices with the truth. It always protects, always trusts, always hopes, always perseveres. (NIV)

Observation

These verses are beautiful but hard to live up to. I know that this has become easier to follow the older I get. It seems that when I was younger, I was much more impatient and easily angered. There was a lot more stress raising children and struggling to make ends meet. It wasn't that I didn't love deeply, but I was sometimes rude and remembered too many offenses. I regret those times deeply and I have asked for forgiveness. What has changed me has been my relationship with the Lord. I have matured as I have read and studied the Bible. This verse gives a description of how I want to be treated, and it gives me a picture of how God loves. This is a verse I need to read often so I will not forget what perfect love is. It should be a goal to work toward as I grow closer to God.

Application

I must make a conscious decision every morning after my prayers to be kind and patient. I need to take a deep breath and let things go. Being rude only makes matters worse and accomplishes nothing. I need to ask God to help with my anger and pride, and to help me forgive the offenses of others. Most of all, I must trust God with what I cannot handle. I need to work toward being true to myself and becoming the kind of person He created me to be.

Prayer

Lord, thank you for being kind and patient with me and for forgiving me for all the times I have been rude and self-seeking. Help me to take your words and fill my heart and mind with them. Help me to forgive and forget the offenses of other people just as you have shown me love and compassion.

In Jesus' name,

Amen

LOVE

Personal S.O.A.P.

Read Romans 12:9-21

Scripture

Romans 12:9-13

Love must be sincere. Hate what is evil; cling to what is good. Be devoted to one another in brotherly love. Honor one another above yourselves. Never be lacking in zeal, but keep your spiritual fervor, serving the Lord. Be joyful in hope, patient in affliction, faithful in prayer. Share with God's people who are in need. Practice hospitality. (NIV)

Observation

Application

Prayer

MONEY

I Timothy 6:9-10

People who want to get rich fall into temptation and a trap and into many foolish and harmful desires that plunge men into ruin and destruction. For the love of money is a root of all kinds of evil. Some people, eager for money, have wandered from the faith and pierced themselves with many griefs. (NIV)

Observation

When my focus turns from God to money I fall into temptation and get myself into difficult situations. Wanting something so badly that it overcomes my ability to discern reality is a driving force that changes me. It is not money that is bad; it is the love of it. I need money to pay my bills and buy groceries, but I am to love God not money. If I have a good job, money in the bank, and the resources to help people, then I am blessed. I sometimes think if I had more money I would be happy. In reality I know that happiness comes from peace and contentment within that only God can give. The grief I bring upon myself by wandering away from my faith will make it very difficult for me to enjoy happiness in my life.

Action

I should regard money as a tool to accomplish something; like a shovel helps me dig a hole. If I can look at money as something I can use to help others I take the "I" out of it and begin to look at it differently. If I get to the point where I will not share my money then I know I have turned away from loving God to loving money. I need to focus my mind on God and depend on Him to guide me.

Prayer

Lord, money is so important in the world that it's easy to lose focus on what is really important. Help me keep my eyes on you and keep me from the temptations that I face every day. Give me the strength to do what is right and glorify you with my earnings, as you continue to give me the ability to work. Thank you for my job and the money you provide. Help me to use it to further your kingdom.

In Jesus' name,

Amen

MONEY

Personal S.O.A.P.

Read Matthew 6:19-34

<u>Scripture</u>

Matthew 6:24

"No one can serve two masters. Either you will hate the one and love the other, or you will be devoted to the one and despise the other. You cannot serve both God and money." (NIV)

<u>Observation</u>

<u>Application</u>

<u>Prayer</u>

PRAYER

Scripture

James 5:16

Therefore confess your sins to each other and pray for each other so that you may be healed. The prayer of a righteous man is powerful and effective. (NIV)

Observation

I believe the scripture is telling me to be so concerned about people that I apologize to them for my sinful behavior. I should also care enough to spend time in prayer for them. If I demonstrate love in this way, I am letting the love of God show through me. I will never know how this positive gesture will affect a life, but God will use it for good.

I must never believe that my prayers are ineffective even though I do not see things change as fast as I think they should. I must stand on His word that says prayers are powerful and effective. I must pray and believe and let God do the rest.

Application

I need to apologize and ask for forgiveness to the people I have offended. I need to pray for others and believe that God will touch their lives and provide protection for them. I will show love and concern in any way that I can.

Prayer

Lord, just as I ask people to forgive me, I ask you to forgive my sins. Fill me with love and compassion. Hear my prayers, Lord. You know the cries of the neglected and abused and those people who live in danger. Please send people to them to show love and mercy and to offer protection. Open the hearts of the lost and help them to come to you.

In Jesus' name,

Amen

PRAYER

Personal S.O.A.P.

Read Ephesians 6:10-20

Scripture

Ephesians 6:18a

And pray in the spirit on all occasions with all kinds of prayers and requests. (NIV)

Observation

Application

Prayer

RIGHTEOUSNESS

I Timothy 6:11-12

But you, man of God, flee from all this, and pursue righteousness, godliness, faith, love, endurance and gentleness. Fight the good fight of the faith. Take hold of the eternal life to which you were called when you made your good confession in the presence of many witnesses. (NIV)

Observation

Righteous: acting in an upright manner; doing what is right; virtuous, moral. This is a tall order in today's society. Righteousness is referred to as goodie-two-shoes behavior until someone wants to hire a good employee, a fair contractor, or elect a politician, and then this behavior is highly desired. This is a virtue God requires of His children. It not only makes my life better because I am free of the guilt of wrong doing, but I can also become a blessing for other people. When I live in this manner, I am able to show God's love to others and they can see God's peace in me. Why is it called the good fight? A good fight is the one you know you will win because you have the best of everything on your side. With God on my side, I will not fear because He will help me overcome my obstacles and lead me to my ultimate reward of eternal life.

Application

I need to stay away from things that take me from a righteous life. I must work to change my behavior to be more of what God wants me to be. I should not let other people tempt me into doing things I know are wrong. I will ask God for strength.

Prayer

Lord, there is temptation all around me. Give me the strength to say no to it so that I can live a life pleasing to you. Help me to be your hands and feet as I go out and make a difference for you. Help people to see your love through me.

In Jesus' name,

Amen

RIGHTEOUSNESS

Personal S.O.A.P.

Read 1 Peter 2:21-25

<u>Scripture</u>

1 Peter 2:24-25

"He himself bore our sins" in his body on the cross, so that we might die to sins and live for righteousness; "by his wounds you have been healed." For "you were like sheep going astray," but now you have returned to the Shepherd and Overseer of your souls. (NIV)

<u>Observation</u>

<u>Application</u>

<u>Prayer</u>

SELFISHNESS

Philippians 2:3-8

Do nothing out of selfish ambition or vain conceit, but in humility consider others better than yourselves. Each of you should look not only to your own interests, but also to the interest of others. Your attitude should be the same as that of Christ Jesus: who being in very nature God, did not consider equality with God something to be grasped, but made himself nothing, taking the very nature of a servant being made in human likeness. And being found in appearance as a man, he humbled himself and became obedient to death even death on a cross. (NIV)

Observation

The phrase that comes to mind when I read this passage is, "my way or the highway." It is the mindset that, "what I have to say or do is more important than your thoughts and needs." When did I get to the point that I became more important than everyone else? In Sunday school I was taught J.O.Y., Jesus first, others second, and yourself last. I believe that if I am serious about changing and following Christ's example, this is a very important first step. How is it possible to worship the Lord when I put myself first? How is it possible to live in peace if I am constantly hurting those around me with my selfish behavior? How is it possible to demonstrate Christ's love if I think so highly of myself? Selfishness is often at the root of every kind of sin.

Application

I need to pray for forgiveness and a changed heart. I must ask the Lord to give me the strength to give up my desire to have everything my way. I need to begin to reach out to people, to listen, to help, and to show love. I need to spend time meditating on scripture and seek out positive role models.

Prayer

Lord, forgive my self-centered ways. Come in and change my heart and give me the strength to overcome my former way of life. Bring me the peace and joy I long to have as I put you first, others second, and myself last.

In Jesus' name,

Amen

SELFISHNESS

Personal S.O.A.P.

Read James 3:13-18

Scripture

James 3:13-16

Who is wise and understanding among you? Let them show it by their good life, by deeds done in the humility that comes from wisdom. But if you harbor bitter envy and selfish ambition in your hearts, do not boast about it or deny the truth. Such "wisdom" does not come down from heaven but is earthly, unspiritual, demonic. For where you have envy and selfish ambition, there you find disorder and every evil practice. (NIV)

Observation

Application

Prayer

WEEKLY REFLECTIONS

Key thoughts from this week's devotions.

DAY 15

_____
_____
_____

DAY 16

_____
_____
_____

DAY 17

_____
_____
_____

DAY 18

_____
_____
_____

DAY 19

_____
_____
_____

DAY 20

_____
_____
_____

DAY 21

_____
_____
_____

SHAME

Hebrews 10: 14-18

Because by one sacrifice he has made perfect forever those who are being made holy. The Holy Spirit also testifies to us about this. First he says: "This is the covenant I will make with them after that time, says the Lord. I will put my laws in their hearts, and I will write them on their minds." Then he adds: "Their sins and lawless acts I will remember no more." And where these have been forgiven, there is no longer any sacrifice for sin. (NIV)

Observation

Jesus was the one true sacrifice for the sins of the world. When I accept Him into my heart and ask for His forgiveness, He will help me remember what I read in His word through the Holy Spirit. I must make a fresh start with my life and forget what happened in the past. He has forgiven my transgressions and forgotten them. There is no need to bear the guilt and shame any longer. I may need to ask people to forgive me and I may need to forgive others, but I can unload years of baggage knowing God has wiped the slate clean. It is up to me to begin to change, to follow His word, and to begin to treat people as God intended. If I let shame wear me down then I am already defeated and I have not fully given it all over to God. I must believe and rest my mind on God's word, or I will never be free.

Application

I must ask for forgiveness and believe God's word. I must begin to meditate on His word for positive reinforcement when shame tries to tempt me to retreat and go backwards. I will put my trust in God for my future and believe that He can help me change.

Prayer

Lord, it is so hard to forget my sins and start over. I need your forgiveness and your help. I know that I cannot do this on my own, so please help other people forgive me and help me to forgive myself. I know that I am a new creation in you and that I cannot change the past, but help me to clear it from my mind. I want to look forward to a new life full of peace and confidence knowing that you are my source for everything.

In Jesus' name,

Amen

SHAME

Personal S.O.A.P.

Read Psalm 34:1-22

<u>Scripture</u>

Psalm 34:5

Those who look to him are radiant; their faces are never covered with shame. (NIV)

<u>Observation</u>

<u>Application</u>

<u>Prayer</u>

SIN ▓▓▓▓▓▓▓▓▓▓▓▓▓▓▓▓▓▓▓▓▓▓▓▓▓▓▓▓

Scripture

I John 1:8-9

If we claim to be without sin, we deceive ourselves and the truth is not in us. If we confess our sins, he is faithful and just and will forgive us our sins and purify us from all unrighteousness. (NIV)

Observation

I know the truth about myself even if I do not want to admit it. Deep down inside I know the ugliness that maybe no one can see, or maybe everyone around me already knows, but I refuse to believe. Either way, God knows. I cannot lie about it any longer if I want to clean up my life. I am human and I sin, but as the scripture says, *He is faithful and just and will forgive.* I cannot become a better person and have a better life unless I deal with my sin. Because more of the same behavior gives me back more of the same in consequences and unhappiness. I am not without hope, because I have the Lord.

Application

I need to stop doing wrong, ask for forgiveness, and resolve to do what is right. I must come clean with myself; evaluate my situation and where my sin has led me. I need to decide what kind of person I really want to be, and then pray that God will send people my way who will help and encourage me. I need to begin to remove myself from tempting situations that cause me to fall back into sin.

Prayer

Lord, I am a sinner and I confess it all to you and ask for your forgiveness. Please help me out of these situations and bring me people who will guide me and encourage me. Give me the strength to walk away from temptation and walk into opportunities that will please you.

In Jesus' Name,

Amen

SIN

Personal S.O.A.P.

Read Psalm 119:1-176

<u>Scripture</u>

Psalm 119:11

I have hidden your word in my heart that I might not sin against you. (NIV)

<u>Observation</u>

<u>Application</u>

<u>Prayer</u>

STUBBORNNESS

Romans 2:4-6

Or do you show contempt for the riches of his kindness, tolerance and patience, not realizing that God's kindness leads you toward repentance? But because of your stubbornness and your unrepentant heart, you are storing up wrath against yourself for the day of God's wrath, when his righteous judgment will be revealed. God "will give to each person according to what he has done." (NIV)

Observation

Stubbornness: refusing to yield, obey, or comply. God pours out His love and mercy on me no matter what I have done. He desires a relationship with His people, so He patiently waits for me to come to Him. Sometimes I may refuse to believe that there is a God or that I need Him in my life. If I am stubborn, I will not be covered by His grace, and I will suffer the consequences of my stubborn heart. A stubborn spirit brings trouble in my life and discord in my relationships. Having a loving relationship with God and other people requires me to be willing to be open and accepting. Stubbornness will cause me much grief and hurt many people around me.

Application

I need to pray for God to help me overcome my stubborn spirit. I must spend time reflecting on how this has affected my personal and spiritual life. I need to try to figure out why this has become such a part of me and how I can begin to open up and let God in. To defeat this stronghold, I must spend time daily studying the Bible for wisdom and guidance.

Prayer

Lord, forgive me for pushing you away. Take me as I am and help me to change. Open my heart so that I am able to receive and give love. Open my mind, so that I can see beyond myself and be open to your calling and to others' needs. Thank you for dying on the cross to save me from my sins and for preparing a place for me with you in eternity.

In Jesus' name,

Amen

STUBBORNNESS

Personal S.O.A.P.

Read Psalm 81:5-16

Scripture

Psalm 81:12-16

So I gave them over to their stubborn hearts to follow their own devices. "If my people would but listen to me, if Israel would follow my ways, how quickly would I subdue their enemies and turn my hand against their foes! Those who hate the LORD would cringe before him, and their punishment would last forever. But you would be fed with the finest of wheat; with honey from the rock I would satisfy you." (NIV)

Observation

Application

Prayer

SUFFERING

Scripture

Roman 5:1-5

Therefore, since we have been justified through faith, we have peace with God through our Lord Jesus Christ, through whom we have gained access by faith into this grace in which we now stand. And we rejoice in the hope of the glory of God. Not only so, but we also rejoice in our suffering because we know that suffering produces perseverance; perseverance, character; and character, hope. And hope does not disappoint us, because God has poured out his love into our hearts by the Holy Spirit, whom he has given us. (NIV)

Observation

Justify: to show to be just and right; free from blame, declare guiltless, acquit, absolve; to prove qualified.

By accepting the grace God has offered me through Jesus Christ, I am forgiven and I am now just and right in the eyes of God. I have a chance at a new life because I am a new creation. I have a reason to rejoice. The truth is that while I am still on earth I will suffer mentally and physically. How I handle those times in my life is a test of my faith in God and will show my true character. I need to pray and not let unbelief (doubt) or confusion prevent God's work in my situation. I must stand on His promises and claim them without hesitation or doubt. If I persevere, I will become stronger and more confident; full of hope. I will give up a worried attitude for a victorious one knowing God will get me through it all.

Application

I need to accept each challenge as an opportunity to grow and rely on God. I must claim His promises, and as I pray, believe without doubting. I need to watch what I say to keep from speaking unbelief over my situation. I must adopt a positive attitude and be determined not to let obstacles get me down. I need to remember the victories and adopt a mind-set of hope and gratitude. I will start a prayer journal so I can look back and see how God has answered my prayers.

<u>Prayer</u>

Lord, I accept your love and grace. Please give me the strength and the knowledge I need to get through this adversity. Renew my troubled mind. Help me to overcome the spirit of unbelief as I put all my trust in you instead of myself.

In Jesus' Name,

Amen

SUFFERING ▰▰▰▰▰▰▰▰▰▰▰▰

Personal S.O.A.P.

Read I Peter 5:6-11

<u>Scripture</u>

I Peter 5:6-7

Humble yourselves, therefore, under God's mighty hand, that he may lift you up in due time. Cast all your anxiety on him because he cares for you. (NIV)

<u>Observation</u>

<u>Application</u>

<u>Prayer</u>

TEMPTATION

Scripture

1 Corinthians 10:13

No temptation has seized you except what is common to man. And God is faithful; he will not let you be tempted beyond what you can bear. But when you are tempted, he will also provide a way out so that you can stand up under it. (NIV)

Observation

There are so many things to tempt me. Some things may tempt one person and never bother another, but there is always something that keeps me walking a tight rope instead of walking on solid ground. My temptations keep me in a state of confusion and stress. I have a way out; a source of strength that non-believer's do not have. I can take comfort in the fact that even when the temptation is strong, God is stronger. When I ask, He will give me the strength to overcome it and get away from the source. God will not let it become more than I can handle. Without Him I fall hard. Even if I do fall, He is there with me through my consequences.

Application

I must pray to God when I am tempted to do the wrong thing, and change my direction and possibly do something to help other people instead. I need to bring forth memorized scripture in my mind and spend time studying the Bible. I must remove the temptation, or remove myself from the source of the temptation. I should not act on impulse, but spend more time thinking about what my consequences could be.

Prayer

Lord, I pray for the strength to overcome these temptations. Help me to find other ways to use my time wisely. Help me to find something good that is so much more enjoyable than what I am tempted to do. Bring people into my life that can be helpful. Thank you for being there for me, and thank you for every blessing you bring my way.

In Jesus' name,

Amen

TEMPTATION

Personal S.O.A.P.

Read Matthew 6:5-15

<u>Scripture</u>

Matthew 6:9-13

This, then, is how you should pray: "Our Father in heaven, hallowed be your name, your kingdom come, your will be done, on earth as it is in heaven. Give us today our daily bread. And forgive us our debts, as we also have forgiven our debtors. And lead us not into temptation, but deliver us from the evil one." (NIV)

<u>Observation</u>

<u>Application</u>

<u>Prayer</u>

THANKFULNESS

I Thessalonians 5:16-18

Be joyful always; pray continually, give thanks in all circumstance; for this is God's will for you in Christ Jesus. (NIV)

Observation

This is a very difficult concept even though it should be easy. Maybe I make this harder than it should be because I want to control everything. Giving thanks in all circumstances would mean that all circumstances are under control and I would not have to worry about them. Some situations are very difficult, but I must make the decision to trust God. I think the key to all this is to pray continually. If I am in constant communication with the Lord, I will be seeking His help and having the confidence that He is taking care of everything. I will be a happier person because I will not be worried and confused; this will make it easier for me to be thankful. Even though the past is over, I tend to replay it in my mind. I must be thankful for the good, empty my mind of the bad, and strive to have a positive purpose for living.

Application

I need to pray, trust, and be thankful for every small detail that I usually overlook as I am hurrying about in my busy life. If I can appreciate the small things, then my thankfulness will become a part of me that will carry me through the tough times. I need to let people know that I am thankful for the things they do. Maybe by doing this I can spread joy and demonstrate thankfulness.

Prayer

Lord, open my eyes to see your creation, love your people, find joy in helping others, and trust you in every aspect of my life. Help me to give you control so I can let go of the joy-robbing fear that comes over me. Help other people see your joy and love in me as I practice thankfulness. Thank you for my family, my friends, and every provision you give, but most of all thank you for dying on the cross for my sins.

In Jesus' name,

Amen

THANKFULNESS

Personal S.O.A.P.

Read Colossians 2:6-10

<u>Scripture</u>

Colossians 2:6-7

So then, just as you received Christ Jesus as Lord, continue to live your lives in him, rooted and built up in him, strengthened in the faith as you were taught, and overflowing with thankfulness. (NIV)

<u>Observation</u>

<u>Application</u>

<u>Prayer</u>

THE BIBLE

Scripture

2 Timothy 3:16-17

All scripture is God breathed and is useful for teaching, rebuking, correcting and training in righteousness, so that the man of God may be thoroughly equipped for every good work. (NIV)

Observation

The Bible is my manual for living. The principles in it, if followed, will provide for me a good life. My creator knows more than I about what works best for me by His design. When I do my own thing against the principles in the Bible I have problems. Just as a parent corrects a child to save them from bad consequences, the scriptures in the Bible correct me and guide me back to the Father. This puts me back on course in my life and in my relationships. I believe He is saying, if I follow His principles I can do His good work. If I turn from His guidance the motivation could turn from being motivated by love, to a self-seeking motivation which could end badly. Just like obeying the laws of the highway to keep me safe, the scriptures in the Bible map out a better route and a safe passage for me through life.

Application

I must ask God to prepare my mind to receive His word then begin to read and study the scriptures and apply the principles to my life. I need to prepare myself for the work ahead and pray for guidance.

Prayer

Lord, help me to understand all that I read in the Bible. Fill me with acceptance and peace as I try to do the right things according to your word. Give me love and patience for others. Please guide my future and show me the way.

In Jesus' name,

Amen

THE BIBLE

Personal S.O.A.P.

Read Romans 15:1-6

Scripture

Romans 15:4

For everything that was written in the past was written to teach us, so that through the endurance taught in the Scriptures and encouragement they provide we might have hope. (NIV)

Observation

Application

Prayer

WEEKLY REFLECTIONS

Key thoughts from this week's devotions.

DAY 22

_____
_____
_____

DAY 23

_____
_____
_____

DAY 24

_____
_____
_____

DAY 25

_____
_____
_____

DAY 26

_____
_____
_____

DAY 27

_____
_____
_____

DAY 28

_____
_____
_____

THE TONGUE

James 3:4-6

Or take ships as an example. Although they are so large and are driven by strong winds, they are steered by a very small rudder wherever the pilot wants to go. Likewise, the tongue is a small part of the body, but it makes great boasts. Consider what a great forest is set on fire by a small spark. The tongue also is a fire, a world of evil among the parts of the body. It corrupts the whole person, sets the whole course of his life on fire, and is itself set on fire by hell. (NIV)

Observation

My speech is something that I do not take time to consider. Sometimes I speak without thinking, and afterward I feel stupid or regret what I said. Unfortunately, this feeling doesn't last long and all too soon I am right back to blurting our garbage again. Yes, the tongue is a hard thing to control. In order to live a peaceful existence I cannot continue to talk in this manner. I will hurt people, cause problems, and sin. This will cause me to live a life full of anxiety and shame. It will never matter what good deeds I do for people, because what I say will negate all my hard work.

Application

I must start a daily devotional time and pray for help with my lack of self control. I need to consider the reasons for the things I say and ask God to help me work through those issues. I must begin to spend more time listening to people instead of thinking about what I want to say next. Most of all, I need to practice compassion, so I will be less likely to hurt people with my words.

Prayer

Lord, forgive me for the terrible things I have said and how I have hurt people. Fill me with compassion for people so that I will care enough to hold my tongue. Help me to use my speech to lift people up instead of tear them down. Help me to become a better listener and friend. Each day I pray that you will keep watch over the things I say while you continue to help me grow strong in you.

In Jesus' name,

Amen

THE TONGUE

Personal S.O.A.P.

Read Proverbs 18:1-24

Scripture

Proverbs 18:21

The tongue has the power of life and death, and those who love it will eat its fruit. (NIV)

Observation

Application

Prayer

TROUBLES

Scripture

Matthew 11:28-29

"Come to me, all you who are weary and burdened, and I will give you rest. Take my yoke upon you and learn from me, for I am gentle and humble in heart, and you will find rest for your souls." (NIV)

Observation

    God is inviting me to come to Him in prayer and lay my problems at His feet. He wants me to trust Him and be able to unload my deepest anxieties. I find myself distraught with problems, but God is there waiting for me to ask Him for help. When I allow myself to let go of these issues, I will free myself of stress. The word yoke means: to join together; link; couple. If I can join myself with the Lord then I can learn from Him and I will find the peace and contentment I need to face my obstacles.

Application

    I must stop worrying so much that I keep myself from sleeping at night. I have to begin to pray and tell God everything. I must allow Him to take control of these circumstances and guide me. I need to take time to meditate on His word and calm my fears as I begin to put my trust in Him.

Prayer

    Lord, I have been letting these problems control my thoughts and deprive me of peace and happiness. Please work through these situations, because I cannot handle them any longer. I put my trust in you and ask you to guide and teach me through this.

In Jesus' Name,

Amen

TROUBLES

Personal S.O.A.P.

Read James 1:2-18

Scripture

James 1:2-4

Consider it pure joy, my brothers and sisters, whenever you face trials of many kinds, because you know that the testing of your faith produces perseverance. Let perseverance finish its work so that you may be mature and complete, not lacking anything. (NIV)

Observation

Application

Prayer

WEEKLY REFLECTIONS

Key thoughts from this week's devotions.

DAY 29

_____
_____
_____

DAY 30

_____
_____
_____

Notes:

_____
_____
_____
_____
_____
_____
_____
_____
_____
_____
_____
_____
_____
_____
_____
_____
_____
_____
_____
_____
_____
_____